A Helpful Change

Alexandra Behr
Illustrations by Carol Strebel

HAMPTON-BROWN

"What are you up to, Ken?" Jana asks her
brother.

"Shhh," Ken says. "I'm going to work on karate
right now." He takes a deep breath, bends his left
leg at the knee, then does a powerful side snap kick
and a swift front snap kick.

"I'm the best in my karate class, you know,"
he brags.

"Oh," Jana says. She thinks Ken is too boastful.

Ken does one more kick, but he is careless and almost hits Jana.

"Be careful!" Jana cries. "You almost kicked me in the head!"

Ken grins. "Why don't *you* try a kick?"

Jana kicks too fast and falls down.

"Ha! That side kick was all wrong," Ken tells her. "It was low and weak, and you didn't stand right. You're hopeless!"

"You're so mean!" Jana says. "I'm going to tell Mom."

Jana goes into the house. "Mom," she complains, "Why does Ken have to say such mean things? I did one bad karate kick and he said I was hopeless."

"That was wrong of Ken," Mom says, "but if you want to get better at karate, why don't you take a class?"

"I don't know," Jana tells her.

"Maybe you will be good at it," Mom says. "You won't know if you don't try."

Jana thinks for a moment. She takes a deep breath. "Okay," she says slowly, "I will try one class."

In class, Jana and
the other kids bow to
the karate teacher.
They bow to show
respect.

The teacher shows the kids how to kneel on the mats. They must put their left knee on the floor, and then their right knee. He tells them to shut their eyes and bow their heads. "Take a slow, deep breath. Try not to think. Let your mind be still," he says.

Jana takes a slow breath. After a little while, she gets up and bows again. She feels peaceful now.

Jana warms up with the
group. First she bends her neck.

"Take your time," the
teacher says. "Be careful."

Jana reaches her hands
straight up, then bends down
to reach the mat.

She sits on the mat with
her legs straight, then reaches
for her toes.

"Now I will teach you how to punch," the teacher says. "There is a right way to punch and a wrong way. I will show you the skillful way."

Jana makes a tight fist with her right hand and punches straight out. Then she punches with her left arm. She punches for what seems like an endless time.

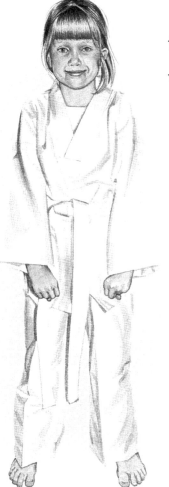

"Now you will try some stances," the teacher says. "A stance is a special way to stand. If you do each stance in the right way, you will look graceful and powerful."

To do the ready stance, Jana stands with her feet about ten inches apart. She holds her fists down low.

To do the left front stance, Jana moves her left leg forward and bends it at the knee. Her right leg is straight. She is careful to do it right.

To do the horse stance, she bends both of her legs. She pretends she is riding a horse. Jana looks at the other kids. Everyone works hard in the soundless room.

"Be mindful of where both feet are when you do the stances," the teacher says. "Try to do each move well. Try to hold each stance for a minute."

At the end of class, the teacher says, "Good work. Remember, it takes a long time to get good at karate. Keep your breath slow. Make your mind peaceful. And most of all, treat everyone as you want to be treated."

At home, Jana thinks about what her teacher said.

"How was class?" Ken says. "Did you fall down?"

"No," Jana says. "In fact, I know something about karate that you don't seem to know, Ken."

"Oh, right!" he says. "What do *you* know that I don't?"

"My teacher says that you have to treat everyone as you want to be treated. You can't be boastful or mean," she replies. "That means you still have lots more work to do." With that, she turns around and walks away.

Ken just stands there, stunned. His sister is right. His own teacher said the same thing last year. How did he forget such an important lesson?

Ken goes out to the back yard. He sees Jana do the stances and the kicks as best she can. She does not look very graceful. He wants to say the stances are wrong, but he stops. Maybe he can be helpful for a change.

Ken says "Jana, can I show you something?"

Jana looks at her brother. Is he offering help or another insult?

Ken keeps talking. "My teacher said that if you don't have a firm stance, your kick will be almost powerless."

"So what should I do?" asks Jana.

"Well, always start with the ready stance," Ken answers.

Jana takes the ready stance.

"For a side snap kick," her brother says, "you will need to lean on your left leg. Then bring your right foot up and rest it on the side of your left knee."

Jana does that, but she wobbles.

"You need to turn your left foot out a little so that you have better balance. Now snap a kick with your right leg!"

Jana kicks, then returns to the ready stance. It works—she doesn't fall over!

20

"I did it! I did it!"
Jana yells. "Thank you,
Ken! You are a great
teacher."

Ken looks surprised, then he slowly smiles. He has enjoyed teaching his sister.

Ken says, "Maybe we can work on karate together. We both have a lot to learn."

"I would like that," Jana tells him.

"Let's tell Mom we both found a helpful way to get better at karate," Ken says, smiling.

"Good idea!" says Jana.

They bow to each other, then go inside the house to see if Mom is making dinner.

THINK ABOUT IT

1. How did Ken change in this story?
   What made him change?

2. What do you think is the hardest part about karate?
   What makes you think so?

3. Tell about something you have worked hard to learn.
   Were you glad you worked so hard?